WIN THESE POSTERS
AND OTHER
UNRELATED PRIZES
INSIDE

Also by Norma Cole

Books & Chapbooks

More Facts (Tente Press)
14000 Facts (a+bend press)
If I'm Asleep (Mermaid Tenement Press)
Where Shadows Will: Selected Poems 1988–2008 (City Lights Books)
Natural Light (Libellum Press)
Collective Memory (Granary Press)
At All (Tom Raworth & His Collages) (Hooke Press)
Do the Monkey (Zasterle Press)
a little a & a (Seeing Eye Books)
Burns (Belladonna Books)
Spinoza in Her Youth (Omnidawn)
Stay Songs, for Stanley Whitney (Bill Maynes Gallery)
The Vulgar Tongue (a+bend press)
Spinoza in Her Youth (A.Bacus)
Desire & its Double (Instress)
Quotable Gestures (CREAPHIS/un bureau sur l'Atlantique)
Mars (CREAPHIS/un bureau sur l'Atlantique)
Capture des lettres et vies du Joker (Format américain/un bureau sur l'Atlantique)
Contrafact (Potes & Poets Press)
Moira (O Books)
Mars (Listening Chamber Editions)
My Bird Book (Littoral Press)
Mon Livre des oiseaux (Foundation Royaumont)
Metamorphopsia (Potes & Poets Press)
Mace Hill Remap (Moving Letters Press)

Translations (Selected)

A Woman With Several Lives, Jean Daive (La Presse)
The Spirit God and the Properties of Nitrogen, Fouad Gabriel Naffah (Post-Apollo Press)
Notebooks, Danielle Collobert (Litmus Press)
Distant Noise, Jean Frémon. With Lydia Davis, Serge Gavronsky, Cole Swenson (Avec Books)
Nude, Anne Portugal (Kelsey Street Press)
Crosscut Universe: Writing on Writing from France (Burning Deck Books)
A Discursive Space: Interviews with Jean Daive (Duration Press)
The Surrealists Look at Art: Essays by Aragon, Breton, Eluard, Soupault, Tzara.
With Michael Palmer (Lapis Press)
It Then, Danielle Collobert (O Books)

Other

SCOUT. Text/image work in CD ROM format (Krupskaya Press)
Catasters Broadside. Collaboration with Jess (Morning Star Editions)

WIN THESE POSTERS
AND OTHER
UNRELATED PRIZES
INSIDE

NORMA COLE

OMNIDAWN PUBLISHING
RICHMOND, CALIFORNIA
2012

Cover art by Amy Trachtenberg
"Glacière," 2011
collage on paper with projection
9 1/2 x 12 1/2 inches

Book cover and interior design by Cassandra Smith

Library of Congress Cataloging-in-Publication Data

Cole, Norma.
Win these posters and other unrelated prizes inside / Norma Cole.
p. cm.
ISBN 978-1-890650-68-1 (pbk. : alk. paper)
I. Title.
PR9199.3.C585W56 2012
811'.54--dc23
                                        2012014453

Published by Omnidawn Publishing, Richmond, California
www.omnidawn.com   (510) 237-5472   (800) 792-4957
10 9 8 7 6 5 4 3 2 1
ISBN: 978-1-890650-68-1

I'd like to thank the editors of Tente Press, a+bend press and Mermaid Tenement Press.

CONTENTS

FACETIME

Santa from a tank, sun over
The minarets
Signs of identity
Soundtrack—by and by

When the morning comes
Heartfelt thanks
One knee bent, the other
Straight out behind, as if

You turn suddenly
Deep into a pirouette
But instead stay still
Then fold to the ground

Arms, legs folded as fact
As it forms
Citation, us
Ephemerally

I like to look at maps
I'll cover you with bees
"Kiss his toe if his hands are bound"
Who said that?

Things of time and space
Salty
___ +___
      audacious

The leaves tremble
Before the anthology of death
And dying, a tautology
Duration generally

Interior flowers
Is this the something else
That sits in neutral space?
Critics email—there are those

Who like to sit in the front
Corner of the restaurant where
Panes of glass meet
Overlapping fragments

Or cosmic rays
Take the Sumerians for example
Land of the Lords of Brightness
Writing, the wheel, the arch and the plow

The water land, Gilgamesh
He who saw the deep
Who became distracted—
Lacunae are great—

Or surpassing all other kings
Any ornament—with the sun
At the center of the circle
Have all the instruments been checked?

14000 FACTS

Be silent with me, as all bells are silent!
Ingeborg Bachmann, "Psalm"

Lower the drawbridge
drawn by dreamers

heat and smoke
no end to jokes

salt on their lands
and salt in the bread

Where did I put my keys?
But aren't we just splinters of stars?

images for argument
the order of nature

or nature of order: this may hurt you
but it won't kill you

Don't wait for me to say anything else.
parched and uneven ground

Don't wait for me
I go

This may hurt me but it won't kill me.

Splinters of stars—and I do
                    I often go back to
                    it was so. And I had
                    from somewhere
                            When I stopped
                    yet ready to so I said

region of unlikeliness
more than a face, solace

The woman
shading her
eyes, standing
at the side of the
road by the tobacco field

tobacco leaves in
rows on racks

a diversion
She observed nothing.

In accordance
(with their nature)

an unaccustomed
form of face

dark gray shades
Did he have leggings on

Or was he Pan? the figure
in rapid motion

to believe
the thought
thinking brought

to the experiment
what you don't
want to believe

(Not the other way round)

thought shards
lined up

little ships
lit up

In the night
a pink cloud

later
in terror

nothing
could be easier

Shadow or cloud
visible aspect

apprehended
source-light

a pillow
of fog

"Richard, he's trying
to kill me"

the crown of letters
fly up and down until they

make a sky she said
without words he said

In this case, the explanation
was the book, the gap

an example that
cannot be written—on that

we all agree, but
what is it like to be a bat

Or the young woman with a
coloring book and a big
box of crayons

purple for flowers
we know what we like

shadows of branches on the shades
and it won't kill us

He mistook "and his banner over me
was love" for "set love in order in me."

no words, no rules, my wildest
dreams, eye to eye, flame, emeralds,
salt—even the sun has cancer

Accommodate—new brains
for old reminds you of

hearing this
in the middle
of a motion picture

diatribe, a regimented set
of actors, a single pixel of data

Broken record or broken heart planning to
journey into the extended dark

forget-me-not
sings sweetly

"tension and dread"
the pirated edition

A sign is a symbol for blood-
soaked arguments.

1 with an axe
2 hacks off "trigger" finger
3 does not go to war

And we thought it said mud
in Babylon or mind's intelligent

field of energy, little aura
veiled as though wrapped

If I were old
To draw water
Like this
As if I were old

In the mouth
in the eyes
what would it be like

to reveal secrets
lilies of the valley, lilacs
ranunculus, sweet peas

do not excite the doves
reaching for night
let me see your face

Lute can mean
her arm becomes

tree branch laden with
mangoes and one hand

to palm the flame
a mortal pain or pang

Their lives are longer
than they look

in those days, we had
the windows open

there was another freezer
under the freezer

Further harmony
falling from the sky
    (arsenic
    lavender oil, meteor
    dust, flakes of gold
    and cinnabar)

disarming
                too close

to
  or something

once heard

The limits of my
language are not
the limits of my

blasted world
the dread
the pink cloud

was flesh
and blood

Was killed at, in
can't quite picture it

border imagination
what's locus?

staring at the fog
startled
                out of

hovering
        oblivion

Sunrise

so far you've
failed to die

           (ruthless)
music   still
at hand or at arm's length

Hermes, the sun
is not ours

Held up at gunpoint
respond with fire

They fished his coat out of the
river and held it up to the fire

to dry. When moved to
speak, you spoke

Slow walking, play
of evening, the silver
ships measuring time

Venus, a sliver
of time
beyond words

The clearing, the light
no gate separates
day and night

more than ever
place of indivisibility

the wolf sees all

Like souls greeting each other
from the windows of eyes

form or harm
turn back any time

snowflakes on a blue
ground

Floating sea ice
as if we'd

seen it just
yesterday

not used to
hearing that

music again

Looked like rain

peremptory music
from the limbic

system—lucky
you're not still

in prison
somewhere

To imagine
a fortress

we're given
a loop

a curveball
come in to play

The manner of their
presentation

aspects of vision "we're
getting killed"

the burning zone
shifts, continuous
carmen, song

See what you
expect, a page

of flames, a cloud
the color of her

old heart, displayed
in a glass case

Fiction: bacon
and eggs in a
parallel universe

smells just as
good

he ran away
as if

the exigency of
is and is not

Potatoes, stones
their living eyes

atoms existing in
unparalleled worlds

as if to turn their
eyes from particular
stars

Techne
crossing the
moon tonight

no one is
sleeping

and yet

MORE FACTS

Four brown birds
fly up into the false
pepper tree

conscious of
mist myself and
outside—when

does the past
begin?

The night's
to imagine not

solve it then
home bed checks
second state

even space does
not repeat

its most welcome

self, standing, her
yellow backpack
waiting at a bus stop

waving at a little
boy in a floppy orange
hat running

towards soldiers, one
a cabinet maker, the other a
barber—*Adieu, mon étoile*

layer of water
body of film
a high first floor

window from which
he jumped

false suns
shining through
ice crystals
what is known
to the senses

myself or outside
the paintings
of flowers
removing
suspicion

some

thing in suspension
that was
is far from

pretending a
circled piece of

air—the fantasy
of being
exempt

from

military service
ultramarine sky
age of treason

supports or contests
breaking news in
the killer's space

the fire or
a day of
sightseeing

where did they
house the horses
anyhow?

undercoat
source of light
the plant

closed. By the
willingness to
stay—he was

distraught, pulling
his shirt, his blue
tie over his face

white orchids

or a wave of
bad checks

BOOM—
nano-weather

smaller buildings
tongue in cheek
the city itself
did not change

on this day
80% of the people
missed each other

cars beyond
bamboo fence
sound of coffee
blueprints
nobody wanted

to hear that

conversation
is just

possible
emptiness is
relative

the way air
resists

the feather

just
the sight
before
the eyes

money

monkey
donkey

hanging on
to sound
Milwaukee

tell me about
the driftless region

compass

compassion
anybody's
lover

clouds
hanging over
the city

rehearsal

for disaster

or disaster
only

a drill—did you
get a new
phone, honey?
are you

practicing
on the corner

in real time

whereas myself
conscious of fog
or outside

flinging beads
into the pond

swim
from one
world

to another
memory
bank

pouring
ashes

into
the violin
case

speak
to the side
don't push

your luck

like diving into
a picture
a real

hotel lobby
in a real
gunshot

silk

illusions

questions
are facts

orange wands
in driving
snow

never

think of
spring

the limit
sun

under the
second sun

second
stutter

small
captions under
these photos

a single
green leaf
rose pink
against

a white
wall

"Existing in the moment means having survived oneself up to that point."
Peter Sloterdijk, *Derrida, An Egyptian*

IF I'M ASLEEP

"…a sheaf of loose, unnumbered sheets"
Felix Fénéon

At the end of the drain, I meant day, I said to the other "Don't come,"
but she insisted. "Don't come back." She wasn't interested.
"You look good," she said, "your handwriting steady. Dignified. Look a
question in the eye. In the face."
"In your face," I said. "Face it. The marathon of everything. Not from
the main action of the film. You comb your hair. If memory leaves no
trace, is it memory? A leaf falls on the tile."
"I didn't see it fall," said the other. "Imagine the shock of a
meadowlark, the ortolan, the phantasm between the sky and my eye,
something that seems like it brushes over. Read obstacle for oracle.
Brush covers it."
"Face up to it, the image, the object," I said. "With our general mind,
my skin's not solid. Happy accident. Seascape with island on the
horizon. Mythology or pathology. We'd like to thank the men and
women. We eat that shit. Mark the starling, the starting point from
which you deviate. If I'm asleep don't wake me."
"I thought I saw," said the other, "a turn, suspense. Where that place is."
"Clear. Your favorite color. Concrete. Hawks the color of sand. Oneiric.
Pull the threads together."

Blackberry bushes besides the freeway. *Ajuga* (bugleweed). Without
leave. Howl, Homer. Sylvia rode up on her bike smiling younger than
springtime. A child is able, hears music as other music.
I wasn't sleeping. The government begins without bees, rocks,
figuring out how much time's gone by by how cold the coffee gets.
Now is the cover of your pen and ink. Names the human project:
earmuffs: shamrocks: a verbal gap. In the early part of the morning a
small hole in the ceiling, a foot pulls up into the hole, ceiling covers
over paradise or charade. You never hear from her. Picking up tissue
from the floor. Transport. They can't stand and shoot. And talk
to each other (even) can't talk to each other, as I said. Up-coming
passages. Epistle of forgiveness: spat on the hair, spat on the faces,
spat on the other foot. Mount Brake-up or Back-up. Heals the words
in her foot. She got plenty. To be or not the little dot bouncing
toward her.

```
I.D.s                 (murderers    )
                      (    &         )
                      (commanders) "it's not about me"
a hole in the sheet, they're
peeping through, secret
police, secret spells


                            TRANSFER


            Nurse|   a hundred octane
            Chico|   totally deserted
            Lito  |   not particularly
dear fred
or
beer bread

They don't have it here

You have a good sleep...
```

(first class) threat or throat
the signs of birds armed with ampersands

a red sign on the breast|
in the form of a duck's | Can I go home now?
foot |

Instead of clambering down the ladder to the beach she stood on the roof watching the glow, glass and water on three sides, beach birds and beach grass. Golden were the doors, one by one the squares turned blue.

Can I go now?

Prepared illuminations for publication: Palace Boom.
Food fight.

Song of Deeds

I was in the fur business in New York and got out
for political reasons. I thought I was killing animals
for a long time, now I must make up for it so I became
a therapist. What is of interest now? "But I am outside"
peeling a Clementine.

Constellations

two feet
the style was likely
to live
to be condemned

no, to be consumed
condensed "as if every"
motion concluded

might be a receiver
(her) appeal to {viewers}
                   {voters }

                                    vast
                                         signature
We couldn't wait even though we didn't know who gave these colors
their names

filtered. Lifted the ability to respond to a glance. The low-hanging
branch. Night is approaching
Butch

one pill less
3 or 4 days—feel it out

no reason to go too
quickly

"Now I know why" you didn't want see the approach. Pink granite
mallet. How to answer the letter? Salt is grammar. "you can hear the
difference between pain and just air." (Carroll Pickett, Death House
Minister)

entire villages

There's still no picture. I don't
Understand it.

Stars arrive. George Oppen's
                        p-----

DOESN'T HAVE ONE

emotions get tired of performance

The difference between a
lyric poem that addresses
a philosophical or
epistemological concern.
line limit 100
*

The Open Book

Before the full
Broken passion heart surgery
An outboard motor
Starts & stops
In place of words
Drowning out
How much we see
And how much
"just air"

United Air
March 6
O'Hare
Buffalo
July 19

<u>wit</u>   <u>rhapsode</u>

<u>luminosity</u>

      refrigerator door—throne
—sit—leave

neck out of
the tin box

spring (moving)
backwards
contrapuntally the (myth)
is a statement
of light
   color
    resists, insists, moves
into senses

air suddenly
distorts
     message

The feeling of all things, especially the wind.

This proves I dreamed.

Norma Cole is a poet, painter and translator. She teaches at the University of San Francisco. Cole has been the recipient of a Wallace Alexander Gerbode Foundation Award, Gertrude Stein Awards, an award from the Fund for Poetry, and an award from the Foundation for Contemporary Arts.

Photo Credit: Robert Eliason

Win These Posters and Other Unrelated Prizes Inside
by Norma Cole

Cover and Interior text set in Cronos Pro.

Cover art by Amy Trachtenberg
"Glacière," 2011
collage on paper with projection
9 1/2 x 12 1/2 inches

Cover and interior design by Cassandra Smith

Omnidawn Publishing
Richmond, California
2012

Ken Keegan & Rusty Morrison, Co-Publishers & Senior Editors
Cassandra Smith, Poetry Editor & Book Designer
Gillian Hamel, Poetry Editor & OmniVerse Managing Editor
Sara Mumolo, Poetry Editor & OmniVerse New-Work Editor
Peter Burghardt, Poetry Editor & Bookstore Outreach Manager
Turner Canty, Poetry Editor & Features Writer
Jared Alford, Facebook Editor
Juliana Paslay, Bookstore Outreach & Features Writer
Craig Santos Perez, Media Consultant